GUMDROPS for MOPPET TOPS

Hey, Teacher!

Dear Teacher,

Hello. My name is Mark Linley, the author and illustrator of the stories in this collection. I am a teacher with eighteen years of teaching experience in the primary grades. I use GUMDROPS for MOPPET TOPS books as a tool in my own classroom, as part of an extensive and well developed systematic early literacy program - a program which I have pieced together and developed myself over the course of my career.

These books have been part of my curriculum for many years and the kids love them. They love the stories, they love the pictures, they love the characters, and they love being able to page through a book and with varying degrees of effort, depending on the child, read every single word. These books work well for children just learning to read, who already know the alphabet and most of the sounds that the letters make. I have personally used these books with pre-kindergartners, kindergartners, beginning first graders, and as extended review for struggling first grade readers. They are easy and appropriate first steps for reading instruction. They will help you to get your students to read.

The GUMDROPS for MOPPET TOPS series was written and illustrated to fill a gap that I saw in the available literature. I created these books because I had students who needed to learn how to blend consonant-vowel-consonant (CVC) words and I was unable to find the right books to address that need. I developed the stories and drew the pictures myself; worked and reworked the drawings by hand and with digital editing software; wrote and rewrote the stories - changing an ending here, moving a page there, discarding stories altogether and writing new ones. These books have gone through many revisions over the years. May they serve you well.

With the GUMDROPS for MOPPET TOPS series, your students will be able read entire books without the frustrating experience of having to puzzle over whether to sound-out a word or to remember it iconically as a sight word. Children feel a sense of accomplishment after successfully reading a page and then moving on to the next page and reading that one too. They feel proud and confident when they are able to read a book by themselves all the way to the end. As a teacher it is a joy to witness the thrill felt by children who have books in their hands that they can read. Finally the kids have books that they can read all the way through!

Enjoy!

Sincerely,

Mark Linley

CONTENTS

The GUMDROPS for MOPPET TOPS Series

CVC Storybooks

15 Reproducible Emergent Reader

Set 3

Stories and Pictures by Mark Linley

bartlebysbox.com

Dedicated to all teachers
and to the children in their care

ISBN 978-0-9977255-2-0

Contact:
Mark Linley
bartlebysbox@gmail.com

PRINTING and ASSEMBLY

1. Copy and Print

For Copy Machines with a Double Sided Printing Option

[OPTION ONE]
Print booklets directly from your GUMDROPS for MOPPET TOPS Blackline Masters Compilation

1. Select two-sided printing on the menu of your copy machine.
2. Open your GUMDROPS for MOPPET TOPS Blackline Masters Compilation to the booklet you wish to print. Scan the page containing the *title page* and *back cover*.
3. Scan the next page in the Compilation, *booklet pages 1* and *10*.
4. Press print to test if both sides of the copy are oriented correctly. If not, re-scan both pages, ensuring that the second page is scanned the other way around.
5. Continue scanning until all pages of your booklet are copied.
6. Press print. All copies will have printed double sided.

[OPTION TWO]
Make MASTER COPIES of your booklets first

1. Copy and print each page of the booklet or booklets your wish to assemble.
2. Place your booklet or booklets in order into the document feeder of your copy machine, *with every other page oriented in the opposite direction*
3. Select the double sided printing option from your machine's menu.
4. Press print. All copies will have printed double sided.

For Copy Machines with a Single Sided Printing Option

A few preliminary *printing tests* will help to determine which way around you must refeed the printed paper for your particular printer or copy machine.

1. Copy and print the odd pages of the booklet you wish to assemble first; print the even pages separately. You will now have two stacks - a stack of odd pages and a stack of even pages.
2. Place the printed odd pages into your copy machine's paper feeder in the direction determined by your printing tests.
3. Place the stack of even pages into the document feeder.
4. Print. Your pages will now be printed double sided.

2. Stack

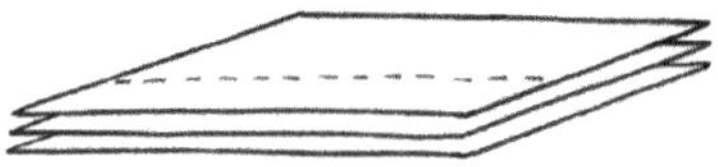

3. Cut

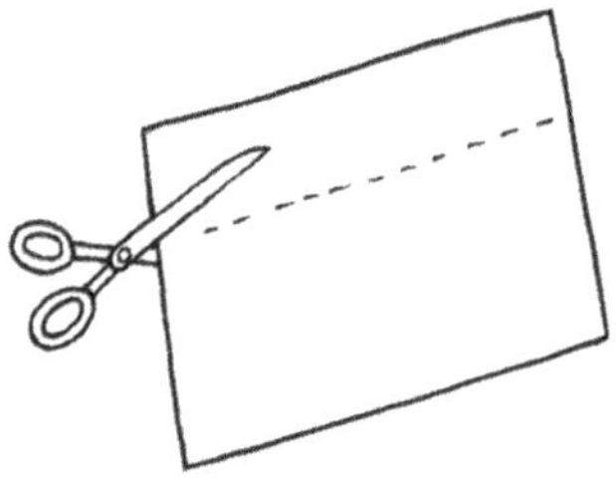

4. Fold and Staple

BOOKLETS

BAGS

gas	pan
up	bag
jug	cub
cup	fun

Got it!

bartlebysbox.com

BAGS

GUMDROPS for MOPPET TOPS SET 3.1

Story and Pictures by Mark Linley

cut

gas

1

fun

10

cut

bag

9

up

2

cut

5

jug

3

cub

8

cut

7

cup

4

cut

pan

5

bag

6

cut

LUV

bud hop
sun run
bug hug
cut

Got it!

bartlebysbox.com

LUV

GUMDROPS for MOPPET TOPS SET 3.1

Story and Pictures by Mark Linley

cut

bud

1

hug

10

cut

mmmmm

9

sun

2

cut

bug

3

run

8

cut

hop

7

cut

4

cut

13

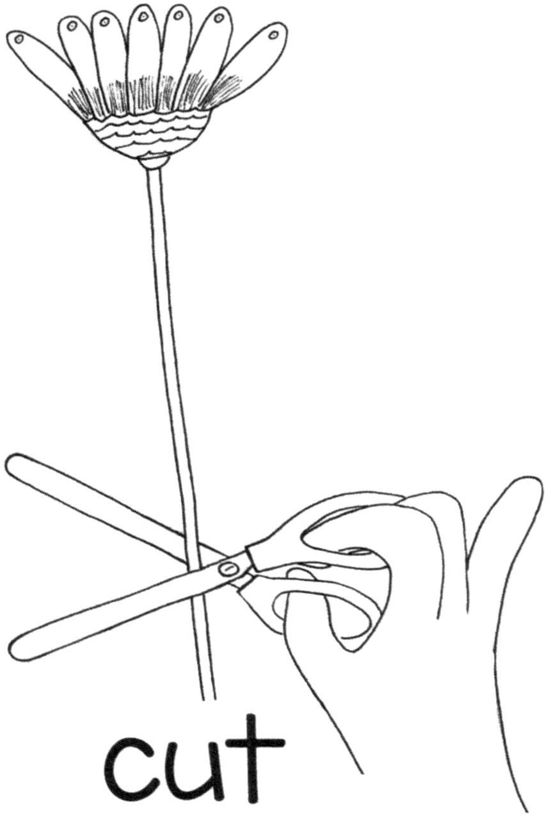

cut

5

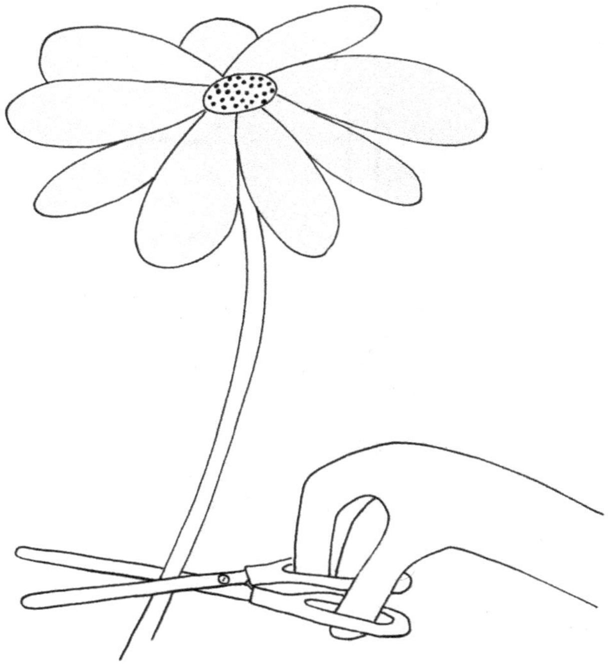

cut

6

cut

JAM

cat	bit
jam	mad
fix	ran
nab	sad

Got it!

bartlebysbox.com

cut

JAM

GUMDROPS for MOPPET TOPS SET 3.1

Story and Pictures by Mark Linley

cat

jam

cut

sad

9

jam

2

cut

fix

3

ran

8

cut

mad

cat

7

4

cut

nab

5

bit

6

cut

HUGS

fun	tub
get	bed
bus	up
pet	yum
hug	

Got it!

bartlebysbox.com

HUGS

GUMDROPS for MOPPET TOPS SET 3.1

Story and Pictures by Mark Linley

cut

fun

1

fun

10

cut

yum

9

get

2

cut

bus

3

up

8

cut

bed

pet

cut

hug

5

tub

6

cut

IT IS WET

wet tip
pen fit
men fix
ten win
hid

bartlebysbox.com

IT IS WET

GUMDROPS for MOPPET TOPS
SET 3.1

Story and Pictures by Mark Linley

cut

wet

wet

cut

win

9

pen

2

cut

men

3

fix

8

cut

fit

7

ten

4

cut

hid

5

tip

6

cut

TAGS

tag pup
bag but
fun sat
hat van

Got it!

bartlebysbox.com

TAGS

GUMDROPS for MOPPET TOPS
SET 3.2

Story and Pictures by Mark Linley

cut

tag

1

van

10

cut

sat

bag

cut

fun

3

but

8

cut

pup

7

hat

4

cut

bag

5

fun

6

cut

MUD

run Mom
mud but
fun job
rug dog

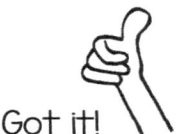

Got it!

bartlebysbox.com

cut

MUD

GUMDROPS for MOPPET TOPS
SET 3.2

Story and Pictures by Mark Linley

run

1

dog

10

cut

job

9

mud

2

cut

fun

3

but

8

cut

mud

7

rug

4

cut

mud

5

Mom

6

cut

YUM

six	mug
mix	sit
in	bun
bib	cut
jug	yum

Got it!

bartlebysbox.com

cut

YUM

GUMDROPS for MOPPET TOPS

SET 3.2

Story and Pictures by Mark Linley

six

1

yum

10

cut

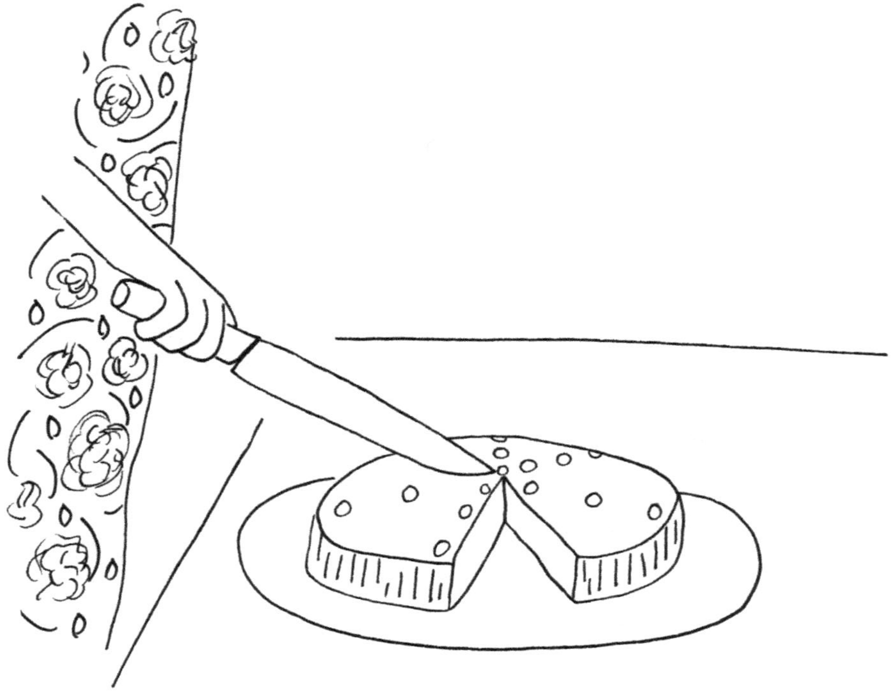

cut

9

mix

2

cut

in

3

bun

8

cut

sit

7

bib

4

cut

jug

5

mug

6

cut

RAT GETS FED

rat	jet
hat	net
ran	mad
get	fed
cat	

Got it!

bartlebysbox.com

cut

RAT GETS FED

GUMDROPS for MOPPET TOPS SET 3.2

Story and Pictures by Mark Linley

rat

fed

1

10

cut

mad

hat

cut

ran

3

net

8

cut

jet

7

get

4

cut

ran

5

cat

6

cut

YES

yes	top
Mom	men
wet	hot
net	box

Got it!

bartlebysbox.com

cut

YES

GUMDROPS for MOPPET TOPS SET 3.2

Story and Pictures by Mark Linley

yes

1

box

10

cut

hot

9

Mom

2

cut

yes

3

yes

8

cut

men

7

wet

4

cut

net

5

top

6

cut

HOT LOGS

log	sit
fix	box
lit	pot
hot	sip

Got it!

bartlebysbox.com

HOT LOGS

GUMDROPS for MOPPET TOPS
SET 3.3

Story and Pictures by Mark Linley

cut

log

1

sip

10

cut

hot

fix

cut

lit

3

hot

8

cut

pot

7

hot

4

cut

sit

5

box

6

cut

GALS

wig	kit
lid	lip
big	hat
zip	bag
hip	sip

bartlebysbox.com

GALS

GUMDROPS for MOPPET TOPS SET 3.3

Story and Pictures by Mark Linley

cut

wig

1

sip

10

cut

bag

lid

9

2

cut

71

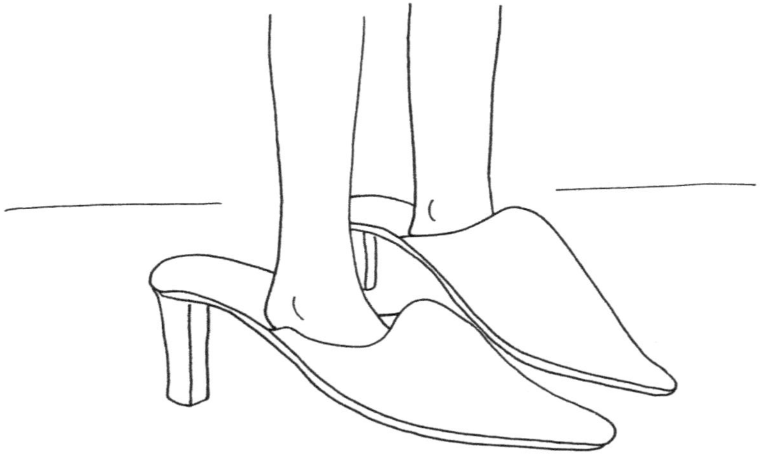

big

3

hat

8

cut

lip

7

zip

4

cut

hip

5

kit

6

cut

BUG

jug ten
cup gum
bug yum
bun up
tub fed

Got it!

bartlebysbox.com

BUG

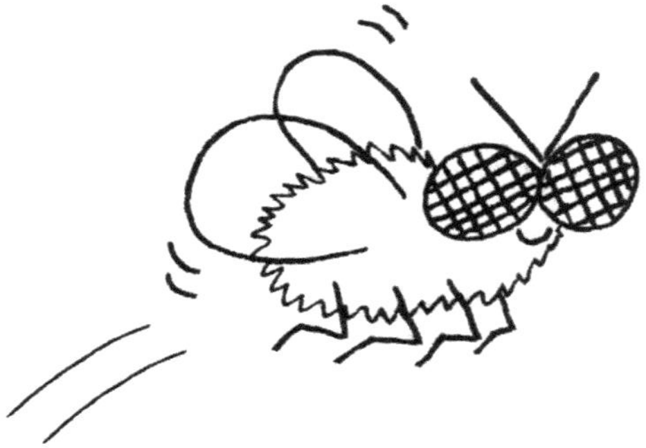

GUMDROPS for MOPPET TOPS
SET 3.3

Story and Pictures by Mark Linley

cut

jug

1

fed

10

cut

up

cup

9

2

cut

bug

3

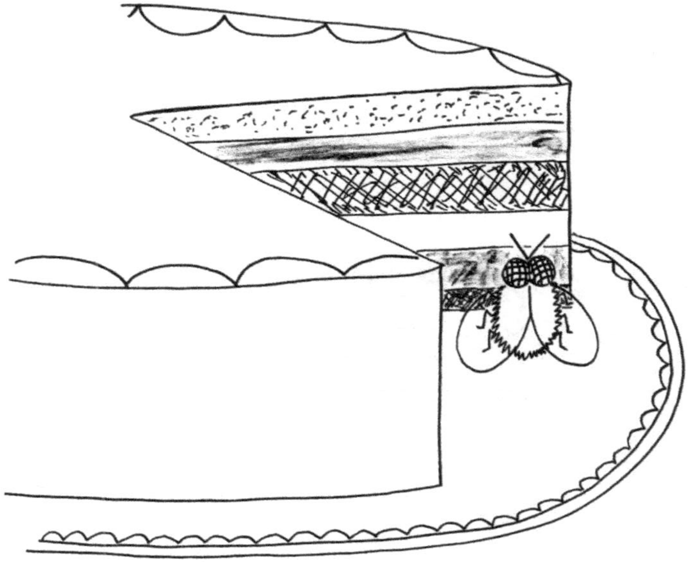

yum

8

cut

gum

7

bun

4

cut

5

ten

6

cut

FIN FUN

pig	in
fin	hid
up	fun

Got it!

bartlebysbox.com

FIN FUN

GUMDROPS for MOPPET TOPS SET 3.3

Story and Pictures by Mark Linley

cut

pig

1

fun

10

cut

fun

9

fin

2

cut

up

3

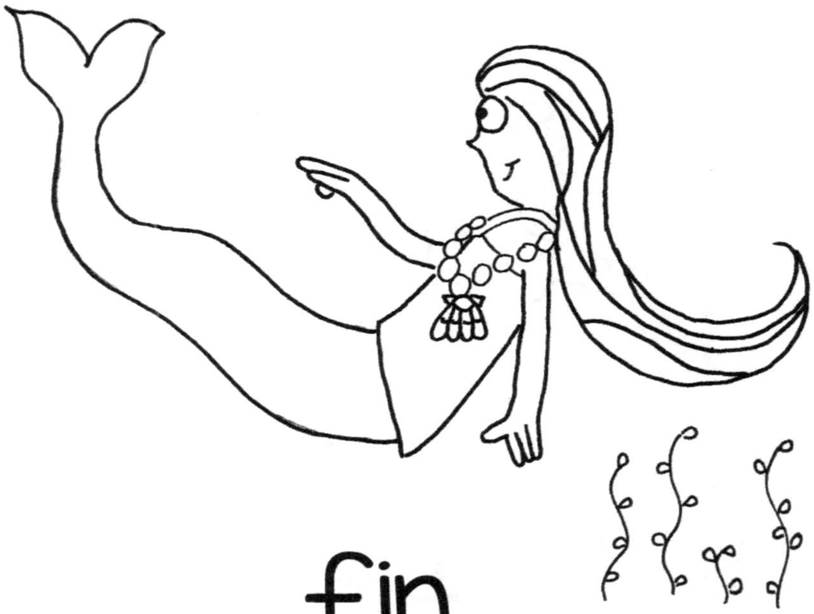

fin

8

cut

fin

7

in

4

cut

in

5

hid

6

cut

JOB

sat	fox
job	lab
bad	pop
box	map

Got it!

bartlebysbox.com

JOB

GUMDROPS for MOPPET TOPS
SET 3.3

Story and Pictures by Mark Linley

cut

sat

1

job

10

cut

map

9

job

2

cut

job

3

pop

8

cut

lab

7

bad

4

cut

box

fox

5

6

cut

LESSON PLANS

Sequence of Instruction

Provided here is a suggested Lesson Plan for teaching CVC decoding in tandem with reading comprehension.

OPENING QUESTIONS

Ask one or more questions from **BEFORE READING** (See **Comprehension Questions**, following)

INTRODUCE the CVC WORDS

PREVIEW the book's CVC words on the board (Use the Back Cover of the book for a list of words)

Procedure for Demonstrating Blending, Sound by Sound

1. Write one CVC word from the book on the board
   - Point to each letter and enunciate the sound of each letter: /c/ - /a/ - /t/
   - Point to the first two letters and enunciate the first two phonemes, then the final consonant: /ca/ - /t/. *Or,* point to the first letter and enunciate the first phoneme, then the medial vowel and final consonant: /c/ - /at/
   - Swipe your finger under the word and blend the entire word: 'cat'
2. Repeat the above sequence as your students chorally read along with you
3. Write the next word, and so on....

READ TOGETHER

GIVE students their own copies of the book
READ each page

For each page, consider doing the following:

1. ENCOURAGE students to look at the picture and make comments
2. ASK questions from **DURING READING** (See **Comprehension Questions**, following)
3. DECODE the page's word
   - Teacher: *Put your finger under the first letter. Ready begin.*
   - Teacher and students: /c/ - /a/ - /t/, /ca/ - /t/
or /c/ - /a/ - /t/, /c/ - /at/
   - Teacher: *What's the word?*
   - Teacher and students: *'cat'*

CONTINUE reading the entire book

CLOSING

DIRECT students to read the words on the Back Cover independently
ASK questions from **AFTER READING** (See **Comprehension Questions**, following)
ASSIGN further study

- Students re-read the book
- Students retell the story to a friend
- Students follow up with GUMDROPS for MOPPET TOPS Independent Practice Worksheets
- Students spell the words with their own letter cards (sets of letters can be made with marker on index cards)
- Students write the words
- Students color the books
- Students take the books home to read with family

Comprehension Questions

Provided here are a variety of questions to ask your students BEFORE, DURING, and AFTER they read. Some teachers may ask many or all of the questions, some teachers only a few. Often one question alone will yeild a rich and lengthy discussion. Many of these questions can be used as writing prompts as well. Of course, a teacher may decide to ask no comprehension questions at all, making their lesson a strictly phonics one.

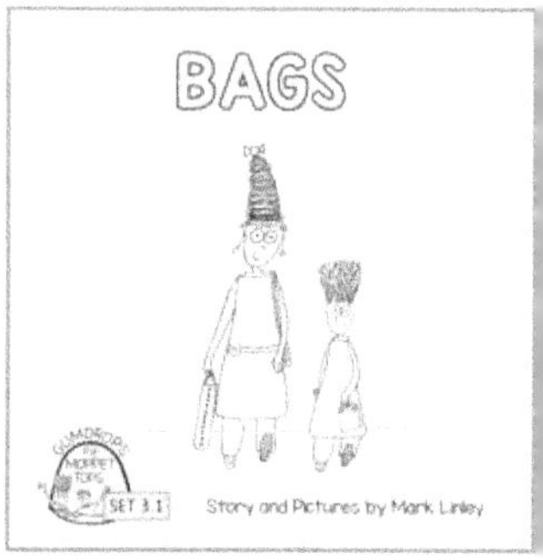

SET 3.1 - Book 1

BAGS

BEFORE READING

Do you like to go shopping?
Where do you go? What kinds of stores do you go to? Who do you go with?
What kinds of things do you buy?
Do you behave yourself while shopping?
What are you allowed to do while you are in a store? What are you not allowed to do?

DURING READING

Title Page — What do you think this story will be about? What might the mom and her daughter have bought? What items might be in their bags?
Page 1 — What is the mom doing? Why do people put gasoline in their cars? Where might the mom and her daughter be going?
Page 2 — What is the girl thinking? What might she be saying to her mom? What is the mom thinking about?
Page 3 — What is happening here?
Page 4 — What is happening here?
Page 5 — What does the mom want to buy? What do people use pans for?
Page 6 — Who is this man? What is his job?
Page 7 — Now where do you think they are going? What kind of machine is this? What does it do? Why do people use escalators?
Page 8 — What is the girl interested in? Do you like stuffed animals? Do you have any stuffed animals? What do you do when you play with stuffed animals? What do you pretend?
Page 9 — Who is this woman? What is her job? What is in the bag?
Page 10 — Are the mom and her daughter enjoying themselves? What do you think might happen next in the story?

AFTER READING

What was this story about? Can you summarize this story?
What were you thinking about as you read this book?
Do you ask your parents to buy you things?
What do you do to get your parents to buy you things?
When you go shopping with your parents, do they let you buy whatever you want?

Comprehension Questions

Provided here are a variety of questions to ask your students BEFORE, DURING, and AFTER they read. Some teachers may ask many or all of the questions, some teachers only a few. Often one question alone will yeild a rich and lengthy discussion. Many of these questions can be used as writing prompts as well. Of course, a teacher may decide to ask no comprehension questions at all, making their lesson a strictly phonics one.

SET 3.1 - Book 2

LUV

BEFORE READING

Why do people give flowers to other people?
Do you like flowers?
Do you like to look at flowers? Do you like to smell them?
Do you know any stories about your parents that happened before you were born? What is love?

DURING READING

Title Page	What is the man holding? What do you think he will do with this bouquet of flowers?
Page 1	What time is it in this picture?
Page 2	Now what time is it? What happened to the flower when the sun came up?
Page 3	Do you like insects? Which ones do you like? Which ones do you dislike? If you were an insect, what kind would you be? Why? What kind would you not like to be?
Page 4	What is happening here?
Page 5	What is happening here?
Page 6	Have you ever picked a flower before? Have you ever picked a bunch of flowers?
Page 7	Have you ever made a bouquet of flowers? Do you know anyone who has received a bouquet of flowers as a present? What is the man doing? How does he feel? What is he thinking about?
Page 8	Now what is the man doing? Why is he running?
Page 9	How does the woman feel? If someone were to give you flowers, how would you feel?
Page 10	Do you have any stories about flowers in your family? Do you have a story you would like to tell about your family?

AFTER READING

What does this story make you think about?
What are some other ways people show their love for one another? What do they say? What do they do?
Who do you love? What do you do for people you love? What do they do for you?

Comprehension Questions

Provided here are a variety of questions to ask your students BEFORE, DURING, and AFTER they read. Some teachers may ask many or all of the questions, some teachers only a few. Often one question alone will yeild a rich and lengthy discussion. Many of these questions can be used as writing prompts as well. Of course, a teacher may decide to ask no comprehension questions at all, making their lesson a strictly phonics one.

SET 3.1 - Book 3

JAM

BEFORE READING

How do you get your food? Who gives it to you? Who makes it for you?

Do you ever get food by yourself? Are you allowed to eat whatever you want out of the refrigerator? What limits do you have?

Do you like to eat jam? What flavors do you like? What do you eat jam with?

Do you know how to make a sandwich? What do you have to do first? What do you do next? And then? (and so on)

DURING READING

Title Page	Why, do you think, does Rat have such a big jar of jam, and such a big knife? What flavor is this jam? (*Teacher: If your kids have read other Rat books, you may want to ask ...* What other stories have we read about Rat? Do you remember what happened?)
Page 1	What is Rat holding in his hand? What is Rat doing?
Page 2	Now what is rat doing? What does he want to do with the jam?
Page 3	What is happening here?
Page 4	What is happening here? How does Rat feel? What do you think will happen next?
Page 5	What is happening here? What does the word 'nab' mean?
Page 6	What is happening here?
Page 7	What is happening here?
Page 8	Where is Rat going? Why is Rat happy?
Page 9	Why doesn't Cat try to get Rat?
Page 10	What happened to Cat? Is Rat safe?

AFTER READING

How much time passes in this story?

What does this book make you think about?

Is Rat a good guy or a bad guy? Is he both good and bad? What do you think?

Is Cat good or bad? Or both? Or neither?

Would you like to live like Rat lives? Why? Why not?

Comprehension Questions

Provided here are a variety of questions to ask your students BEFORE, DURING, and AFTER they read. Some teachers may ask many or all of the questions, some teachers only a few. Often one question alone will yeild a rich and lengthy discussion. Many of these questions can be used as writing prompts as well. Of course, a teacher may decide to ask no comprehension questions at all, making their lesson a strictly phonics one.

SET 3.1 - Book 4

HUGS

BEFORE READING

Do you take care of your toys? What do you do to keep them in good shape?
Do you share your toys with other kids?
Do you make up stories when you play with dolls or action figures? What stories to you act out?

DURING READING

Title Page — What are the girls doing? What are the girls thinking? Do you play with dolls? Do you play with action figures, puppets, or stuffed animals?
Page 1 — Do you see anything strange in this picture? (the dolls have no hair)
Page 2 — What are the girls looking for?
Page 3 — Where are the dolls going on their bus? What story might the girls be acting out?
Page 4 — What will the dolls do with their pet dog?
Page 5 — How do the girls feel about their dolls? What are the girls thinking as they hug their dolls?
Page 6 — Do you wash your toys? Do you have toys that will get ruined if you wash them?
Page 7 — What do you have to do before going to bed? Now what are the girls acting out?
Page 8 — Why are the girls doing this? Do you like to toss your toys up and catch them?
Page 9 — What do you think the girls say to their dolls as they feed them?
Page 10 — What will these girls do next?

AFTER READING

What were you thinking about as you read this book?
Do you like the girls in this book? If so, why do you like them?
How do you play with dolls or action figures, puppets or stuffed animals? What do you do with them that the girls do not do in this book?
If a friend comes over to your house, what do you do together? Do you play different things with different friends? What toys do you play with?
Do you think these girls played well with each other? Did they get along? Did they share? Did they argue?
Is there a lesson or moral to be learned from this story?

Comprehension Questions

Provided here are a variety of questions to ask your students BEFORE, DURING, and AFTER they read. Some teachers may ask many or all of the questions, some teachers only a few. Often one question alone will yeild a rich and lengthy discussion. Many of these questions can be used as writing prompts as well. Of course, a teacher may decide to ask no comprehension questions at all, making their lesson a strictly phonics one.

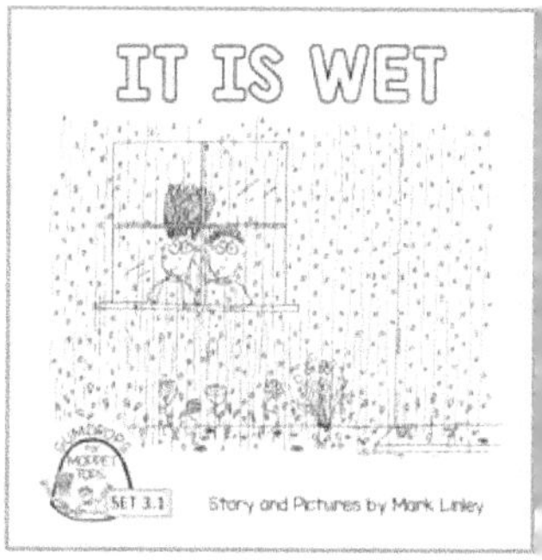

SET 3.1 - Book 5

IT IS WET

BEFORE READING

Do you like rainy days? What is good about rainy days? What is bad about rainy days?
If you have to stay inside all day, what do you do with yourself?
Do you ever go outside and play in the rain?

DURING READING

Title Page	Do these kids like the rain? What are they thinking about?
Page 1	Is it a cold rainy day outside, or is it warm? How do you know this? Have you ever experienced a warm rainy day?
Page 2	What is the boy doing? What do you think the girl will do with the pen?
Page 3	Do you like the picture the boy drew?
Page 4	How high can you count? Do you like hearts? What do hearts make you think about? How do they make you feel?
Page 5	What game are the kids playing?
Page 6	Do you like to build towers with blocks? What is happening here?
Page 7	Do you play with dolls? What is the girl doing with the doll?
Page 8	What is the boy doing? What kind of car is this? (it's remote control) How do you know?
Page 9	Do you like to play with cars? What do you pretend as you play?
age 10	Do you ever watch the rain? Do you ever listen to the rain?

AFTER READING

What do you do on rainy days?
What do you like to do on rainy days that the kids in this book did not do?
Do you have a brother or sister, or a cousin? What indoor activities do you like to play together?
What did this story make you think about?

Comprehension Questions

Provided here are a variety of questions to ask your students BEFORE, DURING, and AFTER they read. Some teachers may ask many or all of the questions, some teachers only a few. Often one question alone will yeild a rich and lengthy discussion. Many of these questions can be used as writing prompts as well. Of course, a teacher may decide to ask no comprehension questions at all, making their lesson a strictly phonics one.

SET 3.2 - Book 1

TAGS

BEFORE READING

Do you go shopping with your mom or dad? Do you like to go shopping?
What kinds of stores do you go to?
Which is your favorite store? If you could buy anything you want there, what would you buy?
Which store do you least like to go to?

DURING READING

Title Page	What is the title of this story? What does the title have to do with the picture? Do you know what a tag is? What are tags used for? What kind of store is this? What do people buy here?
Page 1	What is the mom looking at? Why does she look happy and surprised?
Page 2	What is happening here?
Page 3	What is the girl talking about? What do you talk about with your mom? What do you talk about with your dad? With your grandmother? With your uncle?
Page 4	What is happening here? What do you think the girl is saying to her mom? What is the mom thinking?
Page 5	Now what is the girl saying?
Page 6	What do you think just happened? Where are the tags? Why does the girl look so happy?
Page 7	What is the girl thinking?
Page 8	What is the girl saying to her mom? Why is her mom walking away? What is she thinking?
Page 9	What do you think the mom is saying to her daughter? .
Page 10	Where do you think they are going now? Do you ever fall asleep in the car?

AFTER READING

How much time passes in this story?
Do you think the girl is thankful for what her mom bought her? Are you thankful when your parents buy you things?
What do your parents buy for you? Why is it important to be thankful?
Have you ever bought something for someone else? What was it?
Have you ever made something for someone else? What was it?
If you could give anything at all to another person, what would you give? Who would it be for?

Comprehension Questions

Provided here are a variety of questions to ask your students BEFORE, DURING, and AFTER they read. Some teachers may ask many or all of the questions, some teachers only a few. Often one question alone will yeild a rich and lengthy discussion. Many of these questions can be used as writing prompts as well. Of course, a teacher may decide to ask no comprehension questions at all, making their lesson a strictly phonics one.

SET 3.2 - Book 2

MUD

BEFORE READING

Do you like to play in mud? Do your parents like you to play in mud?
Does it bother you if you get dirty or muddy? Why?
Does it bother your parents if you get dirty or muddy? Why?
What is mud? How does dirt become mud?

DURING READING

Title Page	What do you think this story will be about?
Page 1	What is happening here? Why is the yard so muddy? How did it get so muddy? Does this look fun to you?
Page 2	Do you ever run around in the mud? Do you ever play in the mud? Can you tell a story about a time when you played in the mud, or when you got muddy?
Page 3	What is happening to the boy's shoes? Do you mind if your shoes get muddy? Do your parents mind?
Page 4	What is happening on this page? Do you see a problem about to happen?
Page 5	What is the boy doing? Is there something that the boy does not notice?
Page 6	What is the mom thinking? How is she feeling?
Page 7	What is going on here? What is the boy thinking?
Page 8	What is the mom telling the boy? What is the boy saying?
Page 9	If you got mud all over the rug, what would you do? What would your mom or dad do?
Page 10	Now what is happening? What might happen next in the story?

AFTER READING

What does this story make you think about?
If you could talk to this boy, what would you say to him?
What might the boy have done to keep from making such a mess?
Is there a lesson or moral to be learned from this book?
Can you tell of a time when you got into trouble?
Can you tell of a time when you got into trouble for doing something that you didn't mean to do?

Comprehension Questions

Provided here are a variety of questions to ask your students BEFORE, DURING, and AFTER they read. Some teachers may ask many or all of the questions, some teachers only a few. Often one question alone will yeild a rich and lengthy discussion. Many of these questions can be used as writing prompts as well. Of course, a teacher may decide to ask no comprehension questions at all, making their lesson a strictly phonics one.

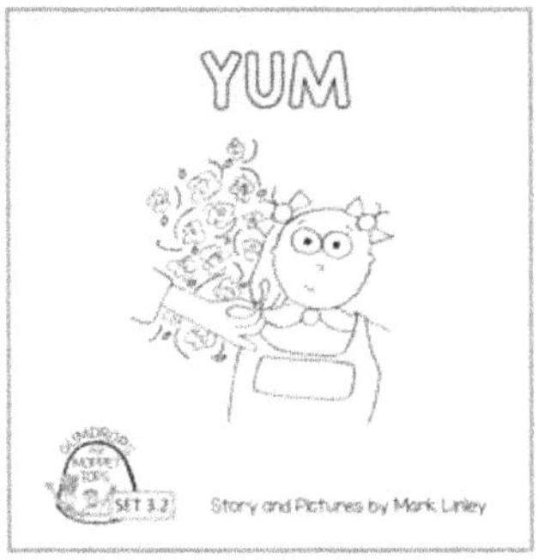

SET 3.2 - Book 3

YUM

BEFORE READING

Does your mom or dad cook? Do they bake? Do they make snacks?
Do you think cooking is a lot of work? What makes you think that?
What is your favorite snack? Is there a snack you like, but do not get to eat very often?

DURING READING

Title Page	What is happening here? Read the title. What do you think this book will be about?
Page 1	What are these?
Page 2	What is happening here? What is the mom making?
Page 3	Now what is the mom doing?
Page 4	Why do babies wear bibs? Do you make a mess when you eat?
Page 5	What is this? What is it used for?
Page 6	What do you think might be in the jug? What do you like to drink?
Page 7	Does your family eat at a table? Where does your family eat?
Page 8	What did the mom make? Would you like to eat this as a snack?
Page 9	Why is the mom cutting the food? Are you allowed to use a sharp knife at home?
Page 10	Where is the dad?

AFTER READING

What is this story about? Can you summarize this story?
How much time passes in this story?
What did you think about as you read this story?
Do you enjoy eating food with your family? What do you talk about?

Comprehension Questions

Provided here are a variety of questions to ask your students BEFORE, DURING, and AFTER they read. Some teachers may ask many or all of the questions, some teachers only a few. Often one question alone will yeild a rich and lengthy discussion. Many of these questions can be used as writing prompts as well. Of course, a teacher may decide to ask no comprehension questions at all, making their lesson a strictly phonics one.

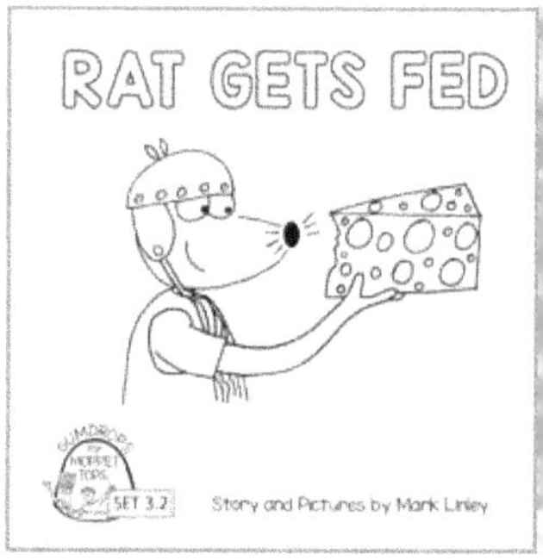

SET 3.2 - Book 4

RAT GETS FED

BEFORE READING

Have you ever been on an airplane?
What types of vehicles have you been on?
Would you ever like to pilot a plane? ride a motorcycle? sail a boat? drive a bus?

DURING READING

Title Page	What is Rat looking at? What is Rat thinking? Why do you think Rat is wearing a helmet on his head?
Page 1	If you could talk to Rat, what would you say to him? What might Rat say to you?
Page 2	What is Rat doing? What is he about to do with his helmet?
Page 3	What is happening here?
Page 4	Do you know what a mouse trap is? Why are mouse traps used? Why are mousetraps a danger for small animals?
Page 5	Did Rat get caught in the mousetrap? Why not?
Page 6	Why does Cat wake up?
Page 7	What do you think Rat will do?
Page 8	Is this cat mean? Why do cats chase mice? Do you think Rat will escape?
Page 9	Why is Cat mad?
Page 10	How does Rat feel? What do you think of Rat? Do you like Rat?

AFTER READING

How much time passes in this story?
How did you feel as you read this book? What did you think about?
Think of Cat and how mad she is at Rat. What is something that makes you angry?
Do you like cheese? Would you do what Rat did to get some cheese?
If you were Rat, would you be afraid of Cat?
If you could talk to Rat, what would you say to him?
If you could talk to Cat, what would you say to her?

Comprehension Questions

Provided here are a variety of questions to ask your students BEFORE, DURING, and AFTER they read. Some teachers may ask many or all of the questions, some teachers only a few. Often one question alone will yeild a rich and lengthy discussion. Many of these questions can be used as writing prompts as well. Of course, a teacher may decide to ask no comprehension questions at all, making their lesson a strictly phonics one.

SET 3.2 - Book 5

YES

BEFORE READING

Do you go on trips with your family? Do you go on day trips? Do you go on over-night trips?
Do you go on long drives in the car? Do you go by train, by boat, by plane?
Do other children come along?
Have you ever been to the beach? If you could go to the beach, how would you get there?
What do people like to do at the beach? What would you do?

DURING READING

Title Page	What do you think about this title? Why is this book called 'Yes'?
Page 1	What are the kids saying? What are they doing?
Page 2	Why are the kids running? Where are they running to?
Page 3	Do you like to play in water? What do you do when you play in water?
Page 4	What are the kids doing?
Page 5	What game is this? Have you ever played volleyball? What are the rules of this game?
Page 6	What is this called? Why are they putting shells on it? Have you ever played in sand? What did you do? Did you build anything?
Page 7	What are these men carrying? What are they about to do?
Page 8	Have you ever flown a kite? Why is the beach a good place to fly a kite?
Page 9	Have you ever dried yourself off in the sun? How does it feel? How can you protect yourself from getting sunburn?
Page 10	What is your favorite snack on a hot day? On a cold day? What might happen next in the story?

AFTER READING

What did you think about as you read this story?
What is your favorite beach activity?
What beach activities can you think of that were not included in this book?
Do you like to play with groups of friends or do you prefer to play with only one friend? Or do you prefer to play alone?
Where would you go if you could go on any trip you wanted to?

Comprehension Questions

Provided here are a variety of questions to ask your students BEFORE, DURING, and AFTER they read. Some teachers may ask many or all of the questions, some teachers only a few. Often one question alone will yeild a rich and lengthy discussion. Many of these questions can be used as writing prompts as well. Of course, a teacher may decide to ask no comprehension questions at all, making their lesson a strictly phonics one.

SET 3.3 - Book 1

HOT LOGS

BEFORE READING

Have you ever been camping?
Have you ever been inside a tent?
Why do people camp?
What do people do when they go camping?
What do you do (if you do go camping)? What would you do (if you could go camping)?

DURING READING

Title Page	Where is the family? How many kids are in this family? What are they looking at?
Page 1	Why do the girl and boy have a log? What is the girl doing? What is she saying? What is the boy doing?
Page 2	What are the kids doing here?
Page 3	What is the father doing?
Page 4	Why do people build campfires?
Page 5	What is happening in this picture? Do you like to sit quietly with your family?
Page 6	What is in this box?
Page 7	What is the father doing?
Page 8	Why is the pot over the fire?
Page 9	Why is the dad wearing a mitt? Is it safe to touch hot pots with your bare hands? How did the pot get hot?
Page 10	Do you like to drink hot drinks? What hot drinks do you like to drink? Does your family like to sit together? Do they talk a lot, or are they mostly quiet? What does your family talk about?

AFTER READING

What were you thinking about as you read this story? Is there anything that you are wondering about? Do you have any questions?
Have you ever sat near a campfire? What do people use fire for?
Is fire dangerous? What can happen?
Have you ever burned yourself? Do you know anyone who has been burned?
Do you and your family ever go places together? Where do you go?

Comprehension Questions

Provided here are a variety of questions to ask your students BEFORE, DURING, and AFTER they read. Some teachers may ask many or all of the questions, some teachers only a few. Often one question alone will yeild a rich and lengthy discussion. Many of these questions can be used as writing prompts as well. Of course, a teacher may decide to ask no comprehension questions at all, making their lesson a strictly phonics one.

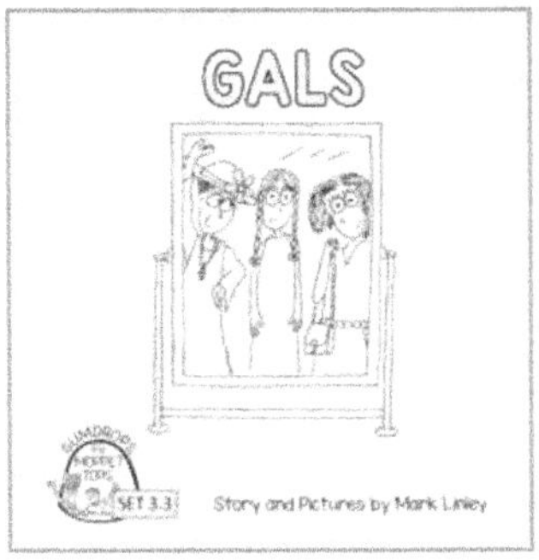

SET 3.3 - Book 2

GALS

BEFORE READING

Do you ever play dress up? What do you pretend?
Do you like to dress up in costumes?
Do your friends (or children of family or family friends) ever come over to your house to play?
Do you ever go over to other people's houses?
What do you play together?

DURING READING

Title Page — What do you think this story is about? What does this title mean? Does this picture make sense? Are the girls in a mirror, or are they looking through a window? Or is it a picture frame?

Page 1 — Have you ever worn a wig before? Do you like to brush your hair or other people's hair? Do you like to braid hair?

Page 2 — Have you ever put on makeup? Do you have adults in your family that use makeup? Are you allowed to use their makeup? Have you ever put on costume makeup for a party or for Halloween?

Page 3 — Have you ever tried on your parent's shoes? Why did you do that?

Page 4 — What is happening here?

Page 5 — Do you wear belts? Why do people wear belts? Why is this girl wearing a belt?

Page 6 — What is in this makeup kit?

Page 7 — What is this girl doing?

Page 8 — Do you like to wear hats? What kind of hat do you like to wear? (Some possible responses: Hard hats, sun hats, rain hats, helmets, baseball hats, uniform hats, hoods, winter hats, swimming caps, fancy hats, straw hats, cowboy hats, ski caps, beanies, bucket hats...)

Page 9 — What is the bag for? What do women put in their purses?

Page 10 — What are the girls doing? What might they talk about? Do you like to have tea parties?

AFTER READING

What did you think about as you read this book?
What is this story about? Can you summarize this book?
What are the girls in this book pretending to be?
How do the girls treat each other in this book?
Is there a lesson or moral to be learned from this book?

Comprehension Questions

Provided here are a variety of questions to ask your students BEFORE, DURING, and AFTER they read. Some teachers may ask many or all of the questions, some teachers only a few. Often one question alone will yeild a rich and lengthy discussion. Many of these questions can be used as writing prompts as well. Of course, a teacher may decide to ask no comprehension questions at all, making their lesson a strictly phonics one.

SET 3.3 - Book 3

BUG

BEFORE READING

Do you like bugs?

Are there some bugs that are good to have around? (Worms are good for the garden, butterflies are beautiful to watch...

What are some bugs that you do not like to have around (or in) your house or apartment?

DURING READING

Title Page	Do you like this bug? Why or why not? What kind of bug is it?
Page 1	What is the fly doing?
Page 2	Is it clean to have a fly land on your cup?
Page 3	What is the fly doing now? Do you think flies like cake?
Page 4	What kind of food is this? Do flies like bread?
Page 5	If the family knew that the fly was on the butter, what would they do?
Page 6	What do you do if there's is a fly in the house? What do your parents do?
Page 7	How do these pictures make you feel?
Page 8	What is the fly thinking?
Page 9	What does the boy think of the fly?
Page 10	Why is the boy mad? Now where will the fly go?

AFTER READING

What did you think about as you read this story?

Do you have any questions? Are you wondering about anything?

How do we keep bugs out of our home? What do your parents do to keep bugs away?

How did you feel as you watched the fly move from food to food? How did the fly feel?

What did this story make you think about?

Comprehension Questions

Provided here are a variety of questions to ask your students BEFORE, DURING, and AFTER they read. Some teachers may ask many or all of the questions, some teachers only a few. Often one question alone will yeild a rich and lengthy discussion. Many of these questions can be used as writing prompts as well. Of course, a teacher may decide to ask no comprehension questions at all, making their lesson a strictly phonics one.

SET 3.3 - Book 4

FIN FUN

BEFORE READING

Have you ever been on a boat? Was it a boat on a lake, a river, an ocean?
Can you swim? What must you wear in the water if you cannot swim? (a floatie)
If you could explore under water in the ocean, what might you find?
What kinds of animals live in the ocean?

DURING READING

Title Page	What does the front cover make you think about? Where is Pig? Why is Pig on a boat? What do you think this story will be about?
Page 1	If you could say something to Pig, what would you say? What might Pig say to you?
Page 2	Look at the picture. Do we know what pig is going to do? Does Pig know how to swim? How do you know? What has Pig put on to help her swim? What does Pig have in her mouth? Do you know what a snorkel is for?
Page 3	Is this what you thought would happen? Have you ever jumped into deep water? Is deep water dangerous? Why?
Page 4	Do you think Pig is safe to dive into deep water?
Page 5	What is in the tank on Pig's back?
Page 6	Who does Pig meet? Do you believe in mermaids?
Page 7	What are they showing each other?
Page 8	Do you think they will become friends?
Page 9	What is happening here?
Page 10	Would you like go diving in the ocean? Do you think you might meet a mermaid? What would you say to her? What would you do with the mermaid? Would you like to meet a mermaid?

AFTER READING

Has Pig made a new friend? Do you like to make a new friends? How do you make friends?
What might happen next in the story?
What did this story make you think about as you read it?
Do you have any questions? Is there anything that you are wondering about?

Comprehension Questions

Provided here are a variety of questions to ask your students BEFORE, DURING, and AFTER they read. Some teachers may ask many or all of the questions, some teachers only a few. Often one question alone will yeild a rich and lengthy discussion. Many of these questions can be used as writing prompts as well. Of course, a teacher may decide to ask no comprehension questions at all, making their lesson a strictly phonics one.

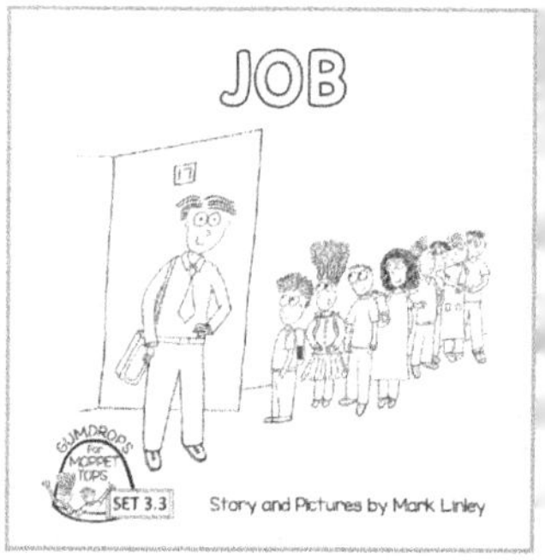

SET 3.3 - Book 5

JOB

BEFORE READING

What do you want to be when you grow up?
What job would you like to do?
Is it important to like your job? Why?
Do people sometimes dislike their jobs? Do people sometimes change their jobs?
What job does your mom or dad do? Have they ever done different jobs?

DURING READING

Title Page	What job do you think this man has? What are these kids like? Where do you think this story takes place?
Page 1	What is happening here? What are the kids doing? Where are they?
Page 2	What are these kids doing? Can you write words like these kids can?
Page 3	Is everyone paying attention here? Is there anyone who is not paying attention? Why is it important to listen to others? What do you think the teacher is telling the students about the fox?
Page 4	What do you think of the fox? What does the teacher think of the fox? What kind of story is the teacher reading? What do you think his book is about?
Page 5	What is the girl doing?
Page 6	Do you like to draw? Do you like to color?
Page 7	What is happening here?
Page 8	What are the kids doing?
Page 9	What is the teacher showing the kids?
Page 10	What games will the kids play outside? What do you like to play when you are outside? What is the teacher thinking? How is he feeling?

AFTER READING

What does this story make you think about?
Do you like this school? How is this school different from your school? How is it the same?
What do you like about your school? What would you like to change about your school?
Does this man like his job? How do you know?
What work would you like to do when you grow up?

INDEPENDENT PRACTICE WORKSHEETS

NAME

DIRECTIONS: Retell the story, trace and write the words.

TRACE WRITE

1.

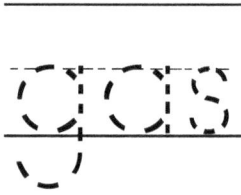

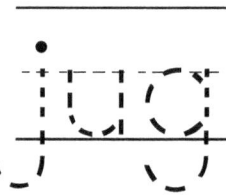

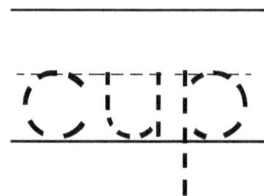

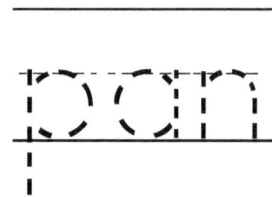

gas

2.

up

3.

jug

4.

cup

5.

pan

bartlebysbox.com

NAME

DIRECTIONS: Retell the story, trace and write the words.

	TRACE	WRITE	
6. 	bag		
7. 	up		
8. 	cub		
9. 	bag		
10. 	fun		

bartlebysbox.com

NAME

DIRECTIONS: Retell the story, trace and write the words.

	TRACE	WRITE
1. 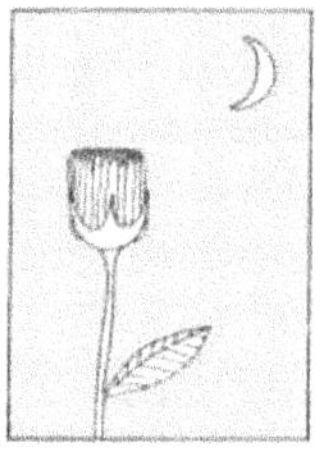	bud	
2. 	sun	
3. 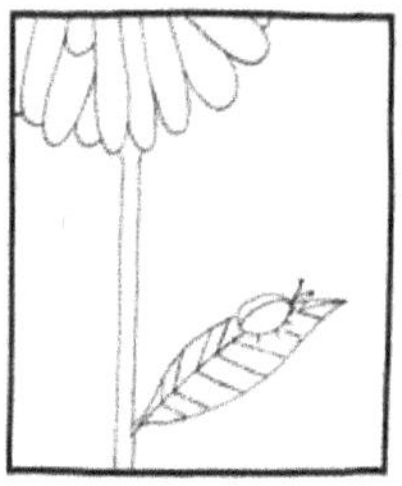	bug	
4. 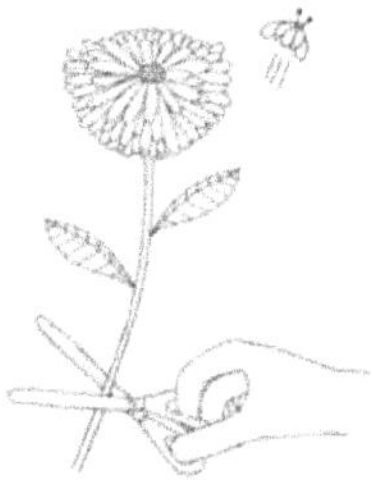	cut	
5. 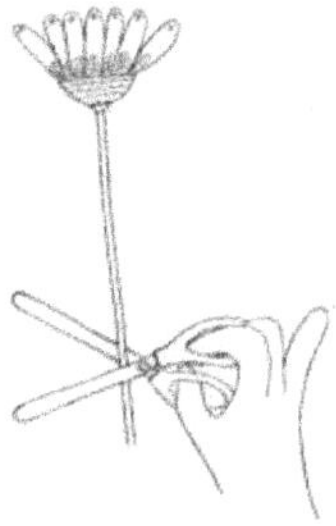	cut	

NAME

DIRECTIONS: Retell the story, trace and write the words.

TRACE WRITE

6. 

cut

7. 

hop

8. 

run

9. 

mmm

10. 

hug

bartlebysbox.com

NAME ______________________

DIRECTIONS: Retell the story, trace and write the words.

	TRACE	WRITE	
1. 	cat		
2. 	jam		
3. 	fix		
4. 	cat		
5. 	nab		

bartlebysbox.com

NAME

DIRECTIONS: Retell the story, trace and write the words.

TRACE | WRITE

6.

bit

7.

mad

8.

ran

9.

sad

10.

jam

NAME

DIRECTIONS: Retell the story, trace and write the words.

	TRACE	WRITE	
1. 	fun		
2. 	get		
3. 	bus		
4. 	pet		
5. 	hug		

NAME

DIRECTIONS: Retell the story, trace and write the words.

TRACE WRITE

6.

tub

7.

bed

8.

up

9.

yum

10.

fun

bartlebysbox.com

NAME

DIRECTIONS: Retell the story, trace and write the words.

TRACE WRITE

1.

wet

2.

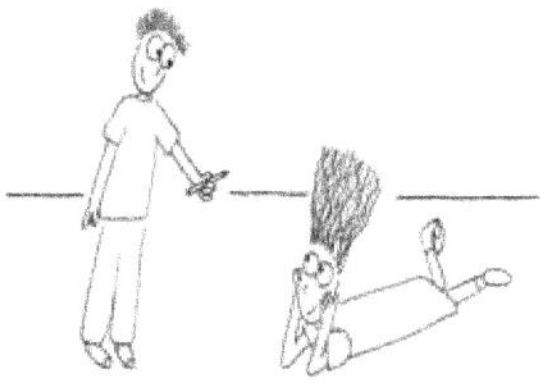

pen

3.

men

4.

ten

5.

hid

IT IS WET

NAME

DIRECTIONS: Retell the story, trace and write the words.

TRACE | WRITE

6.

tip

7.

fit

8.

fix

9.

win

10.

wet

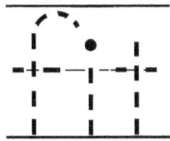

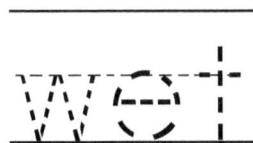

NAME

DIRECTIONS: Retell the story, trace and write the words.

TRACE WRITE

1.

tag

2.

bag

3.

fun

4.

hat

5.

bag

NAME

DIRECTIONS: Retell the story, trace and write the words.

TRACE | WRITE

6.

fun

7.

pup

8.

but

9.

sat

10.

van

NAME ______________________

DIRECTIONS: Retell the story, trace and write the words.

	TRACE	WRITE	
1. 	run		
2. 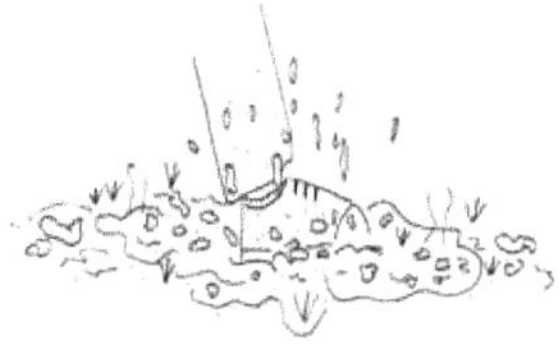	mud		
3. 	fun		
4. 	rug		
5. 	mud		

NAME

DIRECTIONS: Retell the story, trace and write the words.

TRACE | WRITE

6.

Mom

7.

mud

8.

but

9.

job

10.

dog

NAME

DIRECTIONS: Retell the story, trace and write the words.

TRACE WRITE

1.

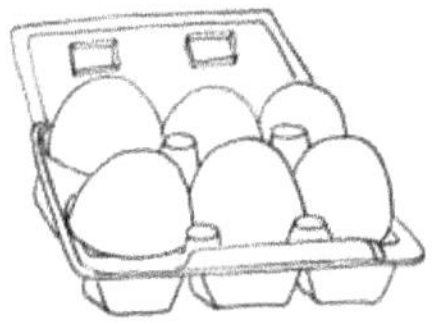

six

2.

mix

3.

in

4.

bib

5.

jug

NAME ______________________

DIRECTIONS: Retell the story, trace and write the words.

	TRACE	WRITE	
6. 	mug		
7. 	sit		
8. 	bun		
9. 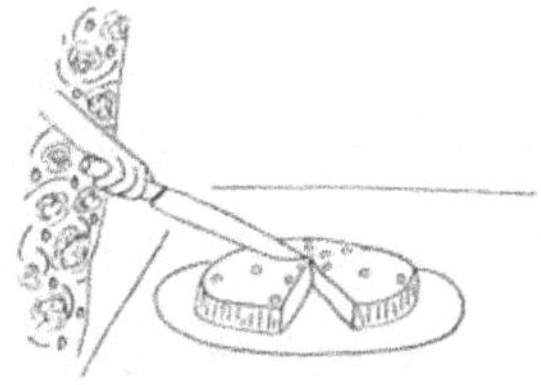	cut		
10. 	yum		

RAT GETS FED

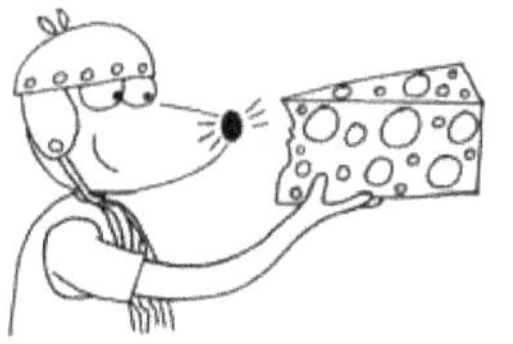

NAME

DIRECTIONS: Retell the story, trace and write the words.

	TRACE	WRITE	
1. 	rat		
2. 	hat		
3. 	ran		
4. 	get		
5. 	ran		

bartlebysbox.com

RAT GETS FED

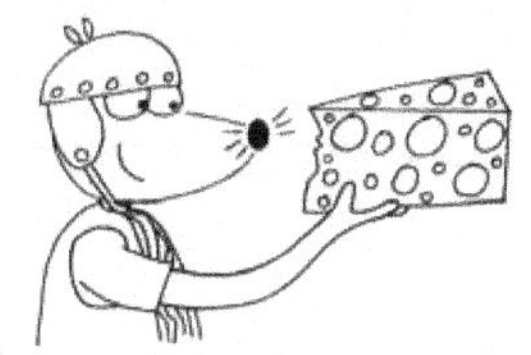

NAME

DIRECTIONS: Retell the story, trace and write the words.

	TRACE	WRITE	
6. 	cat		
7. 	jet		
8. 	net		
9. 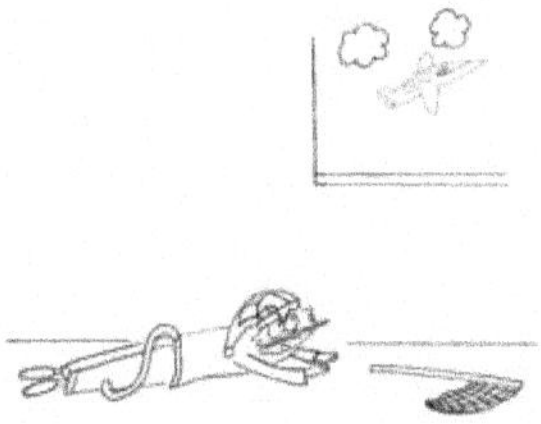	mad		
10. 	fed		

SET 3.2 - Book 4
GUMDROPS FOR MOPPET TOPS

bartlebysbox.com

NAME

DIRECTIONS: Retell the story, trace and write the words.

TRACE | WRITE

1.

yes

2.

Mom

3.

yes

4.

wet

5.

net

bartlebysbox.com

NAME

DIRECTIONS: Retell the story, trace and write the words.

TRACE	WRITE	

6.

top

7.

men

8.

yes

9.

hot

10.

box

bartlebysbox.com

NAME

DIRECTIONS: Retell the story, trace and write the words.

TRACE WRITE

1.

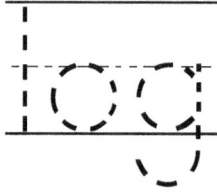

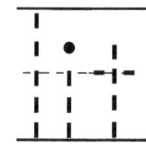

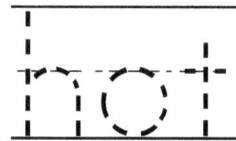

log

2.

fix

3.

lit

4.

hot

5.

sit

NAME

DIRECTIONS: Retell the story, trace and write the words.

TRACE WRITE

6.

box

7.

pot

8.

hot

9.

hot

10.

sip

bartlebysbox.com

NAME

DIRECTIONS: Retell the story, trace and write the words.

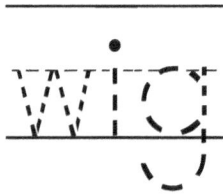

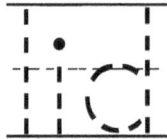

	TRACE	WRITE	
1. 	wig		
2. 	lid		
3. 	big		
4. 	zip		
5. 	hip		

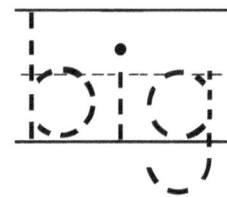

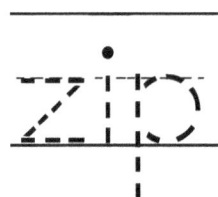

NAME

DIRECTIONS: Retell the story, trace and write the words.

	TRACE	WRITE
6. 	kit	
7. 	lip	
8. 	hat	
9. 	bag	
10. 	sip	

BUG

NAME

DIRECTIONS: Retell the story, trace and write the words.

TRACE WRITE

1.

jug

2.

cup

3.

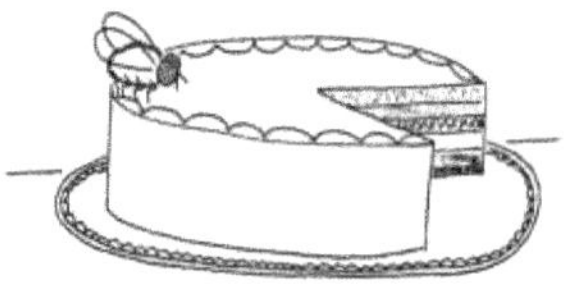

bug

4.

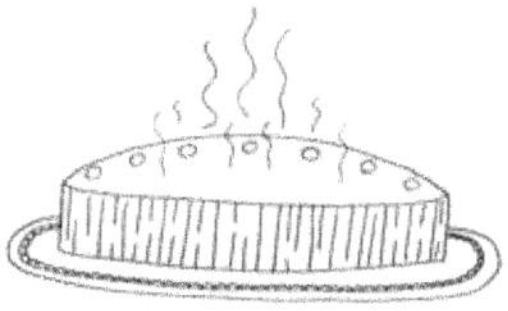

bun

5.

tub

BUG

NAME

DIRECTIONS: Retell the story, trace and write the words.

	TRACE	WRITE
6. 	ten	
7. 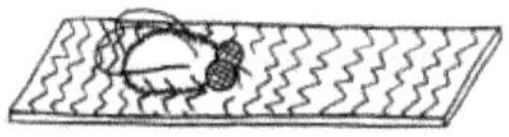	gum	
8. 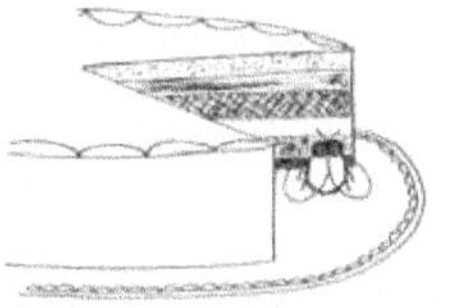	yum	
9. 	up	
10. 	fed	

NAME

DIRECTIONS: Retell the story, trace and write the words.

	TRACE	WRITE	
1. 	pig		
2. 	fin		
3. 	up		
4. 	in		
5. 	in		

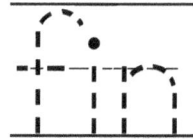

bartlebysbox.com

NAME

DIRECTIONS: Retell the story, trace and write the words.

TRACE WRITE

6.

hid

7.

fin

8.

fin

9.

fun

10.

fun

NAME

DIRECTIONS: Retell the story, trace and write the words.

TRACE WRITE

1.

sat

2.

job

3.

job

4.

fox

5.

box

NAME

DIRECTIONS: Retell the story, trace and write the words.

TRACE WRITE

6.

fox

7.

lab

8.

pop

9.

map

10.

job

SET 3.3 - Book 5
GUMDROPS FOR MOPPET TOPS

bartlebysbox.com

www.ingramcontent.com/pod-product-compliance
Lightning Source LLC
LaVergne TN
LVHW061301060426
835509LV00016B/1660
9780997725520